PUMPKIN & SQUASH
COOKBOOK

Consultant Editor:
Valerie Ferguson

southwater

Contents

Introduction

The eyecatching colours of bright
pumpkins and squashes are a familiar
autumnal sight, following the fresh
greens of the summer courgettes and
marrows. All these are part of the same
family: the squashes, available in a wide
variety of shapes, colours and sizes, all
with their own individual flavours and
textures. Squashes are broadly divided
into summer and winter types:
courgettes and marrows fall into the
summer category, while pumpkins and
butternut and acorn squashes are
examples of winter varieties.

Courgettes and marrows are popular
summer vegetables, but other, less
familiar, summer squashes are also
available; these and the winter varieties
lend themselves to a wealth of creative
dishes both savoury and sweet. Squashes
are easy to prepare and cook and can
be included in simple weekday meals
or stunning dishes for special occasions.
This book is packed with ideas covering
squashes available the whole year through;
try Pumpkin & Pistachio Risotto,
Cumin-spiced Marrow & Spinach and
Courgette & Double-ginger Cake.

Next time your eye is caught by an
unfamiliar squash – perhaps a summer
patty pan or a winter butternut – you
can allow yourself to be tempted to
cook something deliciously different.

Types of Pumpkins & Squashes

There are two kinds of squashes: winter types, which encompass pumpkins and butternut and acorn squashes; and summer types, which include courgettes and marrows.

WINTER SQUASHES
These have tough, inedible skins, dense, fibrous flesh and large seeds. Most winter squashes can be used in both sweet and savoury dishes.

Acorn Squash
Looking rather like a large, slightly ridged acorn, this small to medium-size squash has green or golden skin and orange flesh. It is sweet-flavoured, if a little dry, and is good halved and baked in the oven to serve as a vegetable on its own or filled with a tasty stuffing.

Butternut Squash
This squash resembles a large, elongated pear and has pale-golden skin and bright-orange flesh with a rich, sweet, creamy flavour. Enjoy it roasted, baked and mashed, or in soups or casseroles. The skin is thin enough to be eaten.

Kabocha Squash
This has a thick green-and-orange-tinged skin and dense, deep-orange flesh. It can be used for savoury or sweet dishes.

Pumpkins
With deep-orange skin and flesh, and a roundish shape, pumpkins can reach a vast size, though the smaller ones are sweeter and less fibrous. For the best flavour, choose a ripe pumpkin. They are used in both sweet and savoury dishes, the most notable being pumpkin pie, traditionally served at Thanksgiving in America.

Large pumpkins can be hollowed out to make attractive containers for pumpkin dishes, and of course to make Hallowe'en lanterns. The seeds are edible and highly nutritious.

Turban Squash

Also known as Turk's cap squash, this thick-skinned squash has a smaller top that resembles a turban. Its orange-yellow flesh is slightly sweet and can be baked or boiled and mashed.

SUMMER SQUASHES

Picked when still young, these have thin, edible skins and tender, edible seeds. Their delicate flesh cooks quickly. Mature marrows, however, usually need to have the seeds and skin removed unless they are to be stuffed and baked, when the skin will help them retain their shape.

Courgettes

These widely available summer squashes have a bright-green or yellow skin and creamy-coloured flesh. Small, young ones are the sweetest; larger ones can be slightly bitter. Courgettes are extremely versatile and can be steamed, stir-fried, puréed, baked and used in casseroles and soups. If frying sliced courgettes, and if you have time, sprinkle the slices with salt and leave for at least

30 minutes. Rinse in cold water and pat dry with kitchen paper. Occasionally tiny courgettes are sold with the large, golden flower still attached; the flowers may be stuffed before cooking and are regarded as a delicacy.

Marrows

Although larger than courgettes, marrows are similar in colour and shape. Their flavour is rather bland, so they are best combined with other stronger ingredients: they are good braised or baked with a stuffing or served with a cheese sauce.

Patty Pan Squash

These prettily shaped, white, yellow or green baby squash look like mini-flying saucers. They are best steamed or baked whole to preserve their attractive shape.

Spaghetti Squash

This extraordinary squash has an innocent, marrow-shaped exterior, but its seemingly firm, pale-green flesh separates into long strands after cooking. It is mild-flavoured, juicy and slightly crisp. Eat it baked, straight from the oven, or tossed in a well-flavoured dressing, allowed to cool and incorporated into a salad.

Techniques

Preparing Pumpkins & Other Winter Squashes

Pumpkins and other winter squashes, such as acorn, butternut and kabocha, have a hard rind and central seeds and fibres that should be removed before cooking.

Unless baking in the skin, peel with a large, sturdy knife. Scrape away and discard all the seeds and stringy fibres. Cut the flesh as required.

Cooking Pumpkins & Other Winter Squashes

To bake: halve or cut into serving pieces, leaving on the rind, and score the flesh. Arrange cut-side up in a greased ovenproof dish. Dot with butter.

Bake in a 190°C/375°F/Gas 5 oven for 45 minutes, or until tender.
To boil: drop pieces into boiling salted water and simmer for 4–5 minutes or until tender.
To braise: cut into cubes and cook in a covered pan with 25 g/1 oz/2 tbsp butter and 75 ml/5 tbsp stock or water per 450 g/1 lb for 4–5 minutes or until tender.

To steam: cook cubes in a tightly covered steamer over boiling water until tender.
To roast: Cut into large cubes and roast as you would potatoes.

Serving ideas
(150–225 g/5–8 oz each)
• Add diced apple, a squeeze of lemon juice and 30 ml/2 tbsp soft brown sugar when braising pumpkin. If desired, spice with a little cinnamon and nutmeg or curry powder.
• Bake acorn squash halves with a knob of butter and 5 ml/1 tsp maple syrup in each.

Preparing Courgettes

Courgettes and other thin-skinned summer squashes, such as patty pan, are completely edible, skin and all. Trim the ends from courgettes. Cut, or leave whole, as required.

Cooking Courgettes

To boil: drop into boiling salted water and simmer until tender: 10–12 minutes for whole courgettes, 3–8 minutes for slices.
To braise: cut into diagonal slices and cook as for pumpkins and other winter squashes.

To fry: cook sliced courgettes in butter or oil for 5–10 minutes or until tender and golden brown.
To steam: cook in a covered steamer over boiling water until tender.

Serving ideas
(115–150 g/4–5 oz each)
• Sauté sliced courgettes with finely chopped garlic and chopped fresh parsley and oregano.
• Cut small courgettes in half lengthways and spread the cut surfaces with wholegrain mustard. Grill about 10 cm/4 in from the heat for about 5 minutes or until tender but still firm.

Preparing & Cooking Marrows

To serve as a vegetable accompaniment or to use in soups, peel and cut as required, discarding the seeds. To prepare for stuffing, do not peel, but either cut in half lengthways and scoop out the seeds and some of the flesh, or cut into 5 cm/2 in slices, remove the centre and lay flat to form rings which can be filled.
To boil: drop thick slices into boiling salted water and simmer for 5–8 minutes, or until tender.
To steam: cook thick slices in a covered steamer over boiling water until tender.

Spicy Pumpkin Soup

Ginger and cumin complement the sweet flavour of pumpkin perfectly.

Serves 4

INGREDIENTS
30 ml/2 tbsp olive oil
2 leeks, trimmed and sliced
1 garlic clove, crushed
5 ml/1 tsp ground ginger
5 ml/1 tsp ground cumin
900 g/2 lb pumpkin, peeled and seeded
900 ml/1½ pints/3¾ cups chicken stock
salt and freshly ground black pepper
fresh coriander leaves, to garnish
60 ml/4 tbsp plain yogurt, to serve

1 Heat the oil in a large pan and add the leeks and garlic. Cook gently until softened. Add the ginger and cumin, and cook, stirring, for a further minute.

2 Cut the pumpkin into chunks and add to the pan. Add the stock and seasoning. Bring to the boil and simmer for about 25 minutes, or until the pumpkin is tender. Process the soup, in batches if necessary, in a blender or food processor.

3 Return the soup to the clean pan and reheat. Taste and adjust the seasoning as necessary. Serve in warmed bowls, each with a swirl of yogurt and a garnish of coriander.

COOK'S TIP: For soup bowls, hollow out small squashes and bake for 45 minutes at 180°C/350°F/Gas 4.

Pumpkin Soup with Anise

Liquorice-flavoured anise adds a touch of excitement to this winter soup.

Serves 4

INGREDIENTS
675 g/1½ lb pumpkin, peeled
   and seeded
30 ml/2 tbsp olive oil
2 large onions, sliced
1 garlic clove, crushed
2 fresh red chillies, seeded
   and chopped
5 ml/1 tsp curry paste
750 ml/1¼ pints/3 cups vegetable
   or chicken stock
15 ml/1 tbsp anise
150 ml/¼ pint/⅔ cup single cream
salt and freshly ground
   black pepper

1 Roughly chop the pumpkin. Heat the oil in a large pan and fry the onions until golden. Stir in the garlic, chillies and curry paste. Cook for 1 minute, then add the chopped pumpkin and cook for 5 minutes more.

2 Pour over the stock and season with salt and pepper. Bring to the boil, lower the heat, cover and simmer for about 25 minutes until the pumpkin is tender.

3 Process until smooth in a blender or food processor, then return to the clean pan. Add the anise and reheat. Serve the soup in warmed bowls, adding a spoonful of cream to each portion.

Lamb, Bean & Pumpkin Soup

A really hearty, African-influenced dish with sweet and spicy flavours.

Serves 4

INGREDIENTS
115 g/4 oz/⅔ cup split black-eyed beans,
   soaked for 1–2 hours or overnight
675 g/1½ lb neck of lamb, cut into
   medium-size chunks
5 ml/1 tsp chopped fresh or 2.5 ml/½ tsp
   dried thyme
2 bay leaves
1.2 litres/2 pints/5 cups stock or water
1 onion, sliced
350 g/12 oz pumpkin, peeled,
   seeded and diced
2 black cardamom pods
7.5 ml/1½ tsp ground turmeric
15 ml/1 tbsp chopped fresh coriander
2.5 ml/½ tsp caraway seeds
1 fresh green chilli, seeded and chopped
2 green bananas
1 carrot
salt and freshly ground black pepper

1 Drain the black-eyed beans, place them in a saucepan and cover with fresh cold water. Bring to the boil and boil rapidly for 10 minutes.

2 Reduce the heat and simmer, covered, for 40–50 minutes, or until tender, adding more water if necessary. Remove the pan from the heat and set aside to cool.

3 Meanwhile, put the lamb in a large saucepan, add the thyme, bay leaves and stock or water and bring to the boil. Cover the pan and simmer over a moderate heat for about 1 hour, or until tender.

4 Add the onion, pumpkin, cardamoms, ground turmeric, chopped coriander, caraway, chilli and seasoning, and stir. Bring back to a simmer and cook, uncovered, for 15 minutes, or until the pumpkin is tender, stirring occasionally.

5 When the cooked beans are cool, spoon into a blender or food processor with their liquid and blend to a smooth purée. Stop the machine once and push the beans down the sides of the bowl using a spatula.

6 Peel the bananas and cut into medium slices. Thinly slice the carrot. Stir into the soup with the puréed beans and cook for 10–12 minutes, or until the vegetables are tender. Adjust the seasoning to taste and serve.

Squash à la Grecque

Make sure that you cook these baby squash until they are quite tender, so they can fully absorb the delicious flavours of the marinade.

Serves 4

INGREDIENTS
175 g/6 oz patty pan squash
250 ml/8 fl oz/1 cup white wine
juice of 2 lemons
1 fresh thyme sprig
1 bay leaf
1 small bunch fresh chervil
1.5 ml/¼ tsp coriander seeds, crushed
1.5 ml/¼ tsp black peppercorns,
   lightly crushed
75 ml/5 tbsp olive oil
fresh herbs, to garnish

1 Blanch the patty pan squash in boiling water for 3 minutes and then drain. Refresh them in cold water.

VARIATION: For Courgettes à la Grecque, cut 350 g/12 oz courgettes into 2.5 cm/1 in lengths and cook in the same way, with the addition of three peeled and chopped tomatoes added at step 3.

2 Place the wine, lemon juice, thyme, bay leaf, chervil, coriander, pepper and oil in a pan and add 150 ml/¼ pint/ ⅔ cup water. Bring to the boil and simmer for 10 minutes, covered.

3 Add the patty pan squash and cook for 10 minutes. Remove with a slotted spoon when they are cooked and tender to the bite and place in a wide, shallow serving dish.

4 Reduce the liquid by boiling hard for 10 minutes. Strain it and pour it over the squashes. Leave until cool for the flavours to be absorbed. Serve cold, garnished with fresh herbs.

Butternut Squash & Parmesan Dip

Serve this delicious dip with melba toast or cheese straws.

Serves 4

INGREDIENTS
1 butternut squash
15 g/½ oz/1 tbsp butter
4 garlic cloves, unpeeled
30 ml/2 tbsp freshly grated Parmesan cheese
45–75 ml/3–5 tbsp double cream
salt and freshly ground black pepper

1 Preheat the oven to 200°C/400°F/Gas 6. Halve the butternut squash lengthways, then scoop out and discard the seeds.

2 Use a small, sharp knife to score the flesh deeply in a criss-cross pattern: cut as close to the skin as possible, but take care not to cut through it.

VARIATION: Try making this dip with pumpkin or other types of squash, such as acorn squash or Japanese kabocha.

3 Arrange both halves in a small roasting tin and dot them with the butter. Sprinkle with salt and pepper and bake for 20 minutes.

4 Tuck the unpeeled garlic cloves around the squash in the roasting tin and bake for a further 20 minutes, or until the squash is tender and softened.

5 Scoop the flesh out of the squash shells and place it in a blender or food processor. Slip the garlic cloves out of their skins and add to the squash. Process until smooth.

6 With the motor running, add all but 15 ml/1 tbsp of the Parmesan cheese and then the cream. Adjust the seasoning to taste. Spoon the dip into a serving bowl; it is at its best served warm. Scatter the reserved cheese over the dip.

COOK'S TIP: If you don't have a blender or food processor, simply mash the squash in a bowl using a potato masher, then beat in the grated cheese and cream using a wooden spoon.

Chilled Stuffed Courgettes

Full of flavour, this superb starter is also ideal as a light lunch dish.

Serves 6

INGREDIENTS
6 courgettes
3 tomatoes
1 Spanish onion, very finely chopped
1 garlic clove, crushed
60–90 ml/4–6 tbsp well-flavoured
  French dressing
1 green pepper
15 ml/1 tbsp rinsed capers
5 ml/1 tsp chopped fresh parsley
5 ml/1 tsp chopped fresh basil
salt and freshly ground black pepper
fresh parsley sprigs, to garnish

3 Cut the courgettes in half lengthways. Carefully scoop out the flesh, leaving the shells intact, and chop the flesh into small cubes.

4 Place the courgette flesh in a bowl and cover with half the chopped onion. Dot with the crushed garlic. Drizzle 30 ml/2 tbsp of the dressing over, cover and marinate for 2–3 hours. Wrap the courgette shells tightly in clear film and chill them until they are required.

5 Cut the green pepper in half and remove the core and seeds. Dice the flesh. Chop the tomatoes and capers finely. Stir the green pepper, tomatoes and capers into the courgette mixture, with the remaining onion and the chopped herbs. Season to taste with salt and pepper.

1 Top and tail the courgettes, but do not peel them. Bring a large, shallow pan of lightly salted water to the boil, add the courgettes and simmer for 2–3 minutes, or until they are lightly cooked. Drain well.

2 Plunge the tomatoes in boiling water for 30 seconds. Refresh in cold water, peel and remove the seeds. Set aside.

6 Pour over enough of the remaining dressing to moisten the mixture, and toss well. Spoon the filling into the courgette shells, arrange on a platter and serve garnished with parsley.

Pumpkin Couscous

A traditional Moroccan recipe, partnering pumpkin with tender lamb, dried fruit and spices.

Serves 4–6

INGREDIENTS
75 g/3 oz/½ cup chick-peas, soaked
    overnight
675 g/1½ lb lean lamb, cut into
    bite-size pieces
2 Spanish onions, sliced
pinch of saffron
1.5 ml/¼ tsp ground ginger
2.5 ml/½ tsp ground turmeric
5 ml/1 tsp freshly ground black pepper
450 g/1 lb carrots
675 g/1½ lb pumpkin
75 g/3 oz/⅔ cup raisins
400 g/14 oz/2⅓ cups couscous
salt
fresh parsley, to garnish

1 Drain the chick-peas and cook in plenty of boiling water for 1–1½ hours, or until tender. Drain. Place in a bowl of cold water and remove the skins by rubbing with your fingers. The skins will float to the surface. Discard the skins and drain.

2 Place the lamb, onions, saffron, ginger, turmeric, pepper, salt and 1.2 litres/2 pints/5 cups water in a *couscousière* or large saucepan. Slowly bring to the boil, then cover and simmer for about 1 hour, or until the meat is tender.

3 Meanwhile, prepare the vegetables. Peel or scrape the carrots and cut into 6 cm/2½ in pieces. Peel the pumpkin, discard the skin, seeds and pith, and cut the flesh into 2.5 cm/1 in cubes.

4 Stir the carrots, pumpkin, raisins and chick-peas into the meat mixture, cover the pan and simmer for a further 30–35 minutes, or until the vegetables and meat are completely tender.

5 Prepare the couscous according to the instructions on the packet and spoon on to a large, warmed serving plate, making a well in the centre.

6 Spoon the stew and the gravy into the well, or alternatively stir the stew into the couscous. Extra gravy can be poured into a separate jug. Garnish with parsley and serve.

COOK'S TIP: Because pumpkin and winter squash have mature, hard shells, they can be stored, uncut, in a cool, dry place for several months.

Pumpkin & Parmesan Pasta

Creamy pumpkin with pasta is served with a crunchy garlic topping.

Serves 4

INGREDIENTS
800 g/1¾ lb pumpkin, peeled, seeded
   and cut into small cubes
65 g/2½ oz/5 tbsp butter
15 ml/1 tbsp olive oil
2 garlic cloves, crushed
75 g/3 oz/1½ cups fresh white breadcrumbs
300 g/11 oz tagliatelle
115 g/4 oz rindless smoked back
   bacon, diced
1 onion, sliced
150 ml/¼ pint/⅔ cup single cream
50 g/2 oz/⅔ cup freshly grated
   Parmesan cheese
freshly grated nutmeg
30 ml/2 tbsp chopped fresh
   flat leaf parsley
15 ml/1 tbsp snipped fresh chives
salt and freshly ground black pepper
sprigs of flat leaf parsley, to garnish

1 Bring a large saucepan of water to
the boil. Tip in the pumpkin cubes.
Cook for about 10 minutes, or until
just tender, then drain and set aside.

2 Melt two-thirds of the butter with
the oil in a frying pan. Add the garlic
and breadcrumbs. Fry gently until the
crumbs are golden and crisp. Drain on
kitchen paper and keep warm.

3 Cook the tagliatelle in a large pan
of boiling salted water according to the
packet instructions, or until *al dente.*
Drain and set aside. Heat the remaining
butter in a clean pan and fry the bacon
and onion for 5 minutes. Stir in the
cream and bring to just below boiling
point. Add the pasta and reheat. Stir in
the pumpkin and the remaining
ingredients. Serve sprinkled with
breadcrumbs and garnished with parsley.

Pumpkin & Ham Frittata

A frittata is a substantial Italian-style omelette.

Serves 4

INGREDIENTS
30 ml/2 tbsp sunflower oil
1 large onion, chopped
450 g/1 lb pumpkin, peeled, seeded and cut
    into bite-size pieces
200 ml/7 fl oz/scant 1 cup chicken stock
115 g/4 oz/⅔ cup smoked ham, chopped
6 eggs
10 ml/2 tsp chopped fresh marjoram
salt and freshly ground black pepper

1 Preheat the oven to 190°C/375°F/
Gas 5 and oil a large, shallow
ovenproof dish. Heat the sunflower oil
in a large frying pan and fry the onion
for 3–4 minutes until softened.

2 Add the pumpkin and fry over a
brisk heat for 3–4 minutes, stirring
frequently. Stir in the chicken stock,
cover and simmer over a gentle heat
for 5–6 minutes, or until the pumpkin
is slightly tender. Add the ham.

3 Pour the mixture into the prepared
dish. Beat the eggs with the marjoram
and a little seasoning. Pour into the
dish and bake for 20–25 minutes, or
until the frittata is firm and lightly
golden. Serve hot or warm.

VARIATION: The ham could be
replaced with sliced mushrooms,
quickly fried in a little oil.

Black-eyed Bean Stew with Spicy Pumpkin

For this filling vegetarian dish the pumpkin and beans are cooked separately, each with their own complementary flavourings.

Serves 3–4

INGREDIENTS
225 g/8 oz/1¼ cups black-eyed beans,
   soaked for 4 hours or overnight
1 onion, chopped
1 green or red pepper, seeded and chopped
2 garlic cloves, chopped
1 vegetable stock cube
1 fresh thyme sprig or 5 ml/1 tsp dried thyme
5 ml/1 tsp paprika
2.5 ml/½ tsp ground mixed spice
2 carrots, sliced
15–30 ml/1–2 tbsp vegetable oil
salt and red Tabasco

FOR THE SPICY PUMPKIN
675 g/1½ lb pumpkin
1 onion
25 g/1 oz/2 tbsp butter or margarine
2 garlic cloves, crushed
3 tomatoes, peeled and chopped
2.5 ml/½ tsp ground cinnamon
10 ml/2 tsp curry powder
pinch of freshly grated nutmeg
300 ml/½ pint/1¼ cups water
salt, red Tabasco and freshly ground
   black pepper

1 Drain the beans, place in a pan and cover generously with fresh cold water. Bring to the boil and boil rapidly for 10 minutes.

2 Add the onion, green or red pepper, garlic, stock cube, thyme and spices. Simmer for 40–50 minutes or until the beans are just tender. Season to taste with salt and a little red Tabasco.

3 Add the sliced carrots and vegetable oil and continue cooking the stew over a moderate heat for about 10–12 minutes until the carrots are just cooked, adding a little more water if the stew seems to be a little dry. Remove the saucepan from the heat and set aside.

4 To make the spicy pumpkin, peel the pumpkin, discard the seeds and cut the flesh into 2.5 cm/1 in cubes. Finely chop the onion.

5 Melt the butter or margarine in a large frying pan or saucepan and add the pumpkin, onion, garlic, tomatoes, spices and water. Stir well to combine, and simmer until the pumpkin is soft.

6 Season to taste with salt, Tabasco and ground black pepper. Serve immediately with the black-eyed beans.

COOK'S TIP: Once a pumpkin has been cut, the unused part can be covered closely with clear film and stored in the fridge for up to 4 days.

Cumin-spiced Marrow & Spinach

Tender chunks of marrow with spinach in a creamy, cumin-flavoured sauce. This is a quickly cooked meal, delicious served with rice.

Serves 2

INGREDIENTS
½ marrow, about 450 g/1 lb
30 ml/2 tbsp vegetable oil
10 ml/2 tsp cumin seeds
1 small fresh red chilli, seeded and
  finely chopped
30 ml/2 tbsp water
50 g/2 oz tender young
  spinach leaves
90 ml/6 tbsp single cream
salt and freshly ground
  black pepper
plain or spiced rice, to serve

1 Peel the marrow and cut it in half. Scoop out and discard the seeds. Cut the flesh into bite-size cubes.

2 Heat the oil in a large frying pan. Add the cumin seeds and the chopped chilli. Cook for 1 minute.

3 Add the marrow and water to the pan. Cover with foil or a lid and simmer for 8 minutes, stirring occasionally, until the marrow is just tender. Remove the cover and cook for 2 minutes more or until most of the water has evaporated.

4 Put the young spinach leaves in a colander. Rinse well under cold water, drain and pat dry with kitchen paper. Tear into rough pieces.

5 Add the spinach to the marrow, cover the pan again and cook gently for 1 minute, stirring constantly.

COOK'S TIP: Be careful when handling chillies as the juice can burn sensitive skin. Wear rubber gloves or wash hands thoroughly after preparation.

6 Stir in the cream and cook over a high heat for 2 minutes. Add salt and pepper to taste, and serve immediately with plain or spiced rice.

Butternut Squash & Sage Pizza

The combination of the sweet butternut squash, sage and sharp goat's cheese works wonderfully on this pizza.

Serves 4

INGREDIENTS
15 g/½ oz/1 tbsp butter
30 ml/2 tbsp olive oil
2 shallots, finely chopped
1 butternut squash, peeled, seeded and cubed, about 450 g/1 lb prepared weight
16 fresh sage leaves
450 ml/¾ pint/scant 2 cups thick ready-made tomato sauce
115 g/4 oz mozzarella cheese, sliced
115 g/4 oz firm goat's cheese
salt and freshly ground black pepper

FOR THE PIZZA DOUGH
2.5 ml/½ tsp active dried yeast
pinch of granulated sugar
450 g/1 lb/4 cups strong white flour
5 ml/1 tsp salt
30 ml/2 tbsp olive oil

1 To make the pizza dough, put 300 ml/½ pint/1¼ cups warm water in a measuring jug. Add the yeast and sugar and leave for 5–10 minutes until frothy.

2 Sift the flour and salt into a large bowl and make a well in the centre. Gradually pour in the yeast mixture and the olive oil. Mix to make a smooth dough.

3 Knead the dough on a lightly floured surface for about 10 minutes until smooth, springy and elastic. Place in a floured bowl, cover and leave to rise in a warm place for 1½ hours.

4 Preheat the oven to 200°C/400°F/Gas 6. Oil four baking sheets. Put the butter and oil in a roasting tin and heat in the oven for a few minutes. Add the shallots, squash and half the sage leaves. Toss to coat. Roast for 15–20 minutes until tender.

5 Raise the oven temperature to 220°C/425°F/Gas 7. Divide the pizza dough into four equal pieces and roll out each piece on a lightly floured surface to a 25 cm/10 in round.

6 Transfer each pizza base round to a baking sheet and spread with the tomato sauce, leaving a 1 cm/½ in border all around.

7 Spoon the squash and shallot mixture over the top. Arrange the slices of mozzarella on top of the squash mixture and crumble the goat's cheese over. Scatter with the remaining sage leaves and season with plenty of salt and pepper. Bake for 15–20 minutes until the cheese has melted and the crust on each pizza is golden. Serve immediately.

Pumpkin Gnocchi with a Chanterelle Parsley Cream

Gnocchi is an Italian dumpling usually made from potatoes; in this recipe, pumpkin is added. A chanterelle mushroom sauce provides both richness and flavour. Almond butter is available from health food shops.

Serves 4

INGREDIENTS
450 g/1 lb floury potatoes, cut into
    even chunks
450 g/1 lb pumpkin, peeled, seeded
    and chopped
2 egg yolks
200 g/7 oz/1¾ cups plain flour, plus more
    if necessary
pinch of ground allspice
1.5 ml/¼ tsp ground cinnamon
pinch of freshly grated nutmeg
finely grated rind of ½ orange
salt and freshly ground black pepper
50 g/2 oz shaved Parmesan cheese,
    to serve

FOR THE SAUCE
30 ml/2 tbsp olive oil
1 shallot, chopped
175 g/6 oz/2½ cups fresh chanterelles,
    sliced, or 15 g/½ oz/¼ cup dried,
    soaked for 20 minutes in warm water
10 ml/2 tsp almond butter
150 ml/¼ pint/⅔ cup crème fraîche
a little milk or water
75 ml/5 tbsp chopped fresh parsley

1 Cover the potatoes with cold salted water, bring to the boil and cook for 20 minutes, until tender. Drain.

2 Place the pumpkin in a bowl, cover and microwave on full power for 8 minutes. Alternatively, wrap in foil and bake at 180°C/350°F/Gas 4 for 30 minutes. Drain well.

3 Pass the pumpkin, with the potatoes, through a vegetable mill. Add the egg yolks, flour, spices, orange rind and seasoning, and mix well to make a soft dough. Add more flour if the mixture is too loose.

4 Bring a pan of salted water to the boil. Dredge a work surface with plain flour. Spoon the gnocchi mixture into a piping bag fitted with a 1 cm/½ in plain nozzle. Pipe on to the floured surface to make a 15 cm/6 in sausage.

5 Roll in flour and cut into 2.5 cm/1 in lengths. Repeat the process, making more sausage shapes.

6 Mark each gnocchi lightly with a fork and cook for 3–4 minutes in the boiling water.

7 Meanwhile, to make the sauce, heat the oil in a frying pan, add the shallot and fry until soft without colouring. Add the chanterelles and cook briefly, then add the almond butter.

8 Add the crème fraîche and simmer briefly. Adjust the consistency with milk or water. Add the parsley, and season to taste.

9 Lift the gnocchi out of the water with a slotted spoon, turn into warmed bowls and spoon the sauce over. Serve scattered with Parmesan.

Pumpkin & Pistachio Risotto

Make this elegant combination of creamy golden rice and orange pumpkin as pale or bright as you like by adding different quantities of saffron. Italian arborio rice gives the risotto its authentic consistency.

Serves 4

INGREDIENTS

1.2 litres/2 pints/5 cups vegetable stock
    or water
generous pinch of saffron threads
30 ml/2 tbsp olive oil
1 medium onion, chopped
2 garlic cloves, crushed
450 g/1 lb/2⅓ cups arborio rice
900 g/2 lb pumpkin, peeled, seeded and
    cut into 2 cm/¾ in cubes
200 ml/7 fl oz/scant 1 cup dry
    white wine
15 g/½ oz Parmesan cheese,
    finely grated
50 g/2 oz/⅓ cup pistachio nuts
45 ml/3 tbsp chopped fresh marjoram
    or oregano, plus extra whole leaves
    to garnish
freshly grated nutmeg
salt and freshly ground black pepper

1 Bring the stock or water to the boil and reduce to a low simmer. Ladle a little stock into a small bowl. Add the saffron threads and leave to infuse.

2 Heat the oil in a large saucepan. Add the onion and garlic and cook gently for about 5 minutes until softened. Add the rice and pumpkin and cook for a few more minutes until the rice looks transparent.

3 Pour in the wine and allow it to bubble hard. When it is absorbed add a quarter of the stock and the infused saffron liquid. Stir constantly until all the liquid is absorbed.

4 Gradually add the remaining stock or water a ladleful at a time, allowing the rice to absorb the liquid before adding more, and stirring constantly. After 20–30 minutes the rice should be golden yellow and creamy, and *al dente* when tested.

5 Stir in the grated Parmesan cheese, cover the pan and leave to stand for 5 minutes. To finish, stir in the pistachio nuts and chopped fresh marjoram or oregano leaves. Season to taste with freshly grated nutmeg, salt and black pepper. Scatter over a few whole marjoram or oregano leaves and serve immediately.

Tortelli with Pumpkin Stuffing

Puréed pumpkin and Parmesan cheese fills these small pasta "pillows".

Serves 6–8

INGREDIENTS
1 kg/2¼ lb pumpkin
75 g/3 oz/1½ cups crushed amaretti biscuits
2 eggs
75 g/3 oz/1 cup grated Parmesan cheese
pinch of freshly grated nutmeg
plain breadcrumbs, as required
115 g/4 oz/½ cup butter
salt and freshly ground black pepper
75 g/3 oz/1 cup freshly grated Parmesan
    cheese, to serve

FOR THE EGG PASTA
200 g/7 oz/1¾ cups strong
    plain white flour
pinch salt
2 eggs, beaten
15 ml/1 tbsp olive oil

1 To make the pasta, sift the flour and salt on to a work surface and make a well in the centre. Pour the beaten eggs and oil into the well. Gradually mix the eggs into the flour with the fingers of one hand. Knead the pasta until smooth, wrap and allow to rest for at least 30 minutes.

2 Preheat the oven to 190°C/375°F/ Gas 5. Cut the unpeeled pumpkin into 10 cm/4 in pieces, discarding the seeds. Place the pumpkin pieces in a covered casserole and bake for 45–50 minutes. When cool, cut off the skins.

3 Purée the flesh in a food mill or food processor. Combine with the biscuit crumbs, eggs, Parmesan, nutmeg and seasoning. If the mixture is too wet, add 15–30 ml/1–2 tbsp breadcrumbs. Set aside.

4 Prepare the egg pasta. Roll out very thinly by hand or machine. Do not let the pasta dry out before filling it.

5 Place tablespoons of filling every 6 cm/2½ in along the pasta in rows 5 cm/2 in apart. Cover with another sheet of pasta and press down gently. Use a fluted pastry wheel to cut between the rows to form rectangles with filling in the centre of each.

6 Place the tortelli on a lightly floured surface, and allow to dry for at least 30 minutes, turning them occasionally.

7 Bring a pan of salted water to the boil. Heat the butter over very low heat, taking care that it does not darken.

8 Carefully drop the tortelli into the boiling water. Stir to prevent them from sticking together. They will be cooked in 4–5 minutes. Drain and arrange in individual dishes. Spoon on the melted butter, sprinkle with Parmesan and serve.

Autumn Glory

Glorious pumpkin shells seem too good simply to throw away. Here, one is used as a serving pot for a tasty vegetarian main course.

Serves 4

INGREDIENTS
2 kg/4½ lb pumpkin
1 onion, sliced
2.5 cm/1 in piece fresh root
    ginger, grated
45 ml/3 tbsp extra virgin olive oil
1 courgette, sliced
115 g/4 oz/1⅔ cups mushrooms, sliced
400 g/14 oz can chopped tomatoes
75 g/3 oz/1 cup pasta shells
450 ml/¾ pint/scant 2 cups vegetable stock
60 ml/4 tbsp fromage frais
30 ml/2 tbsp chopped fresh basil
salt and freshly ground black pepper

1 Preheat the oven to 180°C/350°F/ Gas 4. Cut the top off the pumpkin with a large, sharp knife and scoop out and discard the seeds.

2 Using a small, sharp knife and a sturdy tablespoon, extract as much of the pumpkin flesh as possible, then chop it into chunks.

3 Bake the pumpkin shell, with its lid on, in the oven for 45 minutes–1 hour, or until the inside begins to soften.

4 Meanwhile, make the filling. Gently fry the sliced onion, grated ginger and chopped pumpkin flesh in the olive oil for about 10 minutes, stirring occasionally.

5 Add the sliced courgette and mushrooms and cook for a further 3 minutes, stirring once, then add the chopped tomatoes, pasta shells and vegetable stock. Season well, bring to the boil, cover and simmer gently for 10 minutes.

6 Stir the fromage frais and basil into the pasta, spoon the mixture into the pumpkin shell and serve. (It may not be possible to fit all the filling into the shell; serve the rest separately if this is the case.)

Lamb-stuffed Squash

This recipe is ideal for using any leftover cooked meat and rice. The baked squash are served with a creamy tomato sauce.

Serves 6 as a main course, 12 as a starter

INGREDIENTS
6 acorn squash, halved
45 ml/3 tbsp lemon juice
25 g/1 oz/2 tbsp butter
30 ml/2 tbsp plain flour
250 ml/8 fl oz/1 cup whipping cream
175 ml/6 fl oz/¾ cup passata
115 g/4 oz/½ cup crumbled feta cheese
    and fresh basil leaves, to garnish,
    plus extra to serve

FOR THE FILLING
350–450 g/12 oz–1 lb cooked lean lamb,
    cut into strips
175 g/6 oz/1½ cups cooked
    long grain rice
25 g/1 oz/2 tbsp butter, melted
25 g/1 oz/½ cup fresh breadcrumbs
50 ml/2 fl oz/¼ cup milk
30 ml/2 tbsp finely grated onion
30 ml/2 tbsp chopped fresh parsley
2 eggs, beaten
salt and freshly ground
    black pepper

1 Preheat the oven to 180°C/350°F/ Gas 4. Trim the bases of the squash, if necessary, so that they will stand up securely. Using a teaspoon, remove the insides of the squash, leaving a layer of flesh about 1 cm/½ in thick. Take care not to cut the outer skin or base.

2 Blanch the squash in boiling water with the lemon juice for 2–3 minutes, then plunge them into cold water. Drain well and leave to cool.

3 Meanwhile, to make the filling, place the cooked lamb and rice, the butter, breadcrumbs, milk, onion, parsley, eggs and seasoning in a bowl and mix well. Place the squash in a lightly greased ovenproof dish and fill them with the lamb mixture.

4 Put the butter and flour in a pan. Whisk in the whipping cream and bring to the boil, whisking all the time. Cook for 1–2 minutes until thickened, then season well. Pour this sauce over the prepared squash, then pour over the passata.

5 Bake the squash in the oven for 25–30 minutes. To serve, drizzle them with a little of the sauce and sprinkle with feta cheese and basil leaves. Serve separately any extra sauce, feta and basil.

Stuffed Acorn Squash with Parmesan

For this dish the oven-baked flesh of the squash is mixed with butter, pine nuts and Parmesan cheese, then returned to the shell.

Serves 4

INGREDIENTS

2 acorn or butternut squash, about
   450 g/1 lb each
15 ml/1 tbsp olive oil
50 g/2 oz/¼ cup butter, melted
75 g/3 oz/1 cup freshly grated
   Parmesan cheese
60 ml/4 tbsp pine nuts, toasted
2.5 ml/½ tsp freshly grated nutmeg
salt and freshly ground black pepper
shavings of Parmesan cheese, to garnish

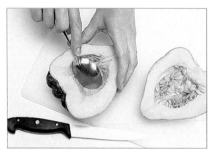

1 Preheat the oven to 180°C/350°F/ Gas 4. Cut the squash in half and scoop out the seeds. Brush the cut surface with oil, and season.

VARIATION: Spaghetti squash can also be cooked in this way. Scoop out the spaghetti-like strands and toss with the filling mixture.

2 Place the squash in a single layer in a greased ovenproof dish, cover and bake in the oven for 25–30 minutes, or until tender.

3 Remove the squash from the oven and scoop out the flesh, leaving the skin intact. Dice the flesh and place in a bowl.

4 Stir in the melted butter. Add the grated Parmesan cheese, toasted pine nuts, salt and freshly ground black pepper. Toss well to mix evenly.

5 Spoon the mixture back into the squash shells and sprinkle with grated nutmeg. Reheat briefly in the oven, if you wish, before serving sprinkled with shavings of Parmesan cheese.

Baked Butternut Squash with Sweetcorn

A creamy, sweet and nutty filling makes the perfect topping for tender, buttery squash. Serve these delightful squash on a bed of salad leaves for a delicious autumnal meal.

Serves 4

INGREDIENTS

2 butternut or acorn squash, about
 500 g/1¼ lb each
15 ml/1 tbsp olive oil
175 g/6 oz/1 cup canned sweetcorn
 kernels, drained
115 g/4 oz/scant ½ cup unsweetened
 chestnut purée
75 ml/5 tbsp plain yogurt
50 g/2 oz/¼ cup fresh goat's cheese
salt and freshly ground
 black pepper
snipped fresh chives,
 to garnish

1 Preheat the oven to 180°C/350°F/ Gas 4. Cut the squash in half lengthways using a large heavy knife, scoop out the seeds with a spoon and discard them.

2 Place the squash halves on a baking sheet and brush the flesh lightly with the olive oil. Bake in the oven for 25–30 minutes, or until tender.

3 In a bowl, mix together the sweetcorn, chestnut purée and yogurt. Season to taste with salt and pepper.

4 Remove the squash halves from the oven and divide the chestnut mixture among them, spooning it into the hollows.

5 Top each half with a quarter of the goat's cheese and return to the oven for a further 10–15 minutes. Garnish with chives and serve.

VARIATION: Use mozzarella or other mild, soft cheeses in place of goat's cheese.

Courgette & Dill Tart

Sliced courgettes with a hint of fresh dill in a crisp pastry case.
This summer tart is easy to prepare and tastes simply wonderful.

Serves 4

INGREDIENTS
115 g/4 oz/1 cup plain wholemeal flour
115 g/4 oz/1 cup self-raising flour
pinch of salt
115 g/4 oz/½ cup unsalted butter, chilled
   and diced
75 ml/5 tbsp ice-cold water
1 fresh dill sprig, to garnish

FOR THE FILLING
15 ml/1 tbsp sunflower oil
3 courgettes, thinly sliced
2 egg yolks
150 ml/¼ pint/⅔ cup double cream
1 garlic clove, crushed
15 ml/1 tbsp finely chopped
   fresh dill
salt and freshly ground black pepper

1 Sift the flours into a bowl,
returning to the bowl any of the
wheat bran remaining in the sieve,
then place in a food processor. Add
the salt and butter and process,
using the pulse button, until the
mixture resembles fine breadcrumbs.
Alternatively, rub the mixture together
using the fingertips.

2 Gradually add the water until the
mixture forms a dough. Do not over-
process. Wrap in clear film and place
in the fridge for 30 minutes to rest.

3 Preheat the oven to 200°C/400°F/
Gas 6 and grease a 20 cm/8 in flan tin.
Roll out the pastry and, draping it
over the rolling pin, ease into the tin.
Prick the base with a fork and bake
"blind" for 10–15 minutes until lightly
browned. If it rises slightly while
baking press down gently with a fork.

4 Meanwhile, to make the filling, heat
the oil in a frying pan and sauté the
courgettes for 2–3 minutes until
lightly browned, turning occasionally.

5 Blend the egg yolks, double cream,
garlic and dill in a small bowl. Season
to taste with salt and pepper.

6 Line the pastry case with layers of courgette slices and gently pour over the cream mixture. Return to the oven for 25–30 minutes or until the filling is firm and lightly golden. Cool in the tin, then remove before serving, garnished with a dill sprig.

Potato & Pumpkin Pudding

Serve this savoury pudding with any meat dish or simply with a salad.

Serves 4

INGREDIENTS
45 ml/3 tbsp olive oil
1 garlic clove, sliced
675 g/1½ lb pumpkin flesh, cut into
   2 cm/¾ in chunks
350 g/12 oz cooked potatoes
25 g/1 oz/2 tbsp butter
90 g/3½ oz/scant ½ cup ricotta cheese
50 g/2 oz/⅔ cup grated Parmesan cheese
pinch of freshly grated nutmeg
4 medium eggs, separated
salt and freshly ground black pepper
chopped fresh herbs, to garnish

1 Preheat the oven to 200°F/400°F/
Gas 6. Grease a 1.75 litre/3 pint/
7½ cup, shallow, oval baking dish.

2 Heat the oil in a large pan, add the
garlic and pumpkin and cook for
15–20 minutes or until tender. Place
the pumpkin and potatoes in a large
bowl and mash well with the butter.

3 Mash the ricotta with a fork until
smooth and add to the mixture. Stir in
the Parmesan, nutmeg and seasoning.
Add the egg yolks, one at a time, until
mixed thoroughly.

4 In a grease-free bowl whisk the
egg whites until they form stiff peaks,
then fold gently into the pumpkin
mixture. Spoon into the prepared
baking dish and bake for 30 minutes
until golden and firm. Serve garnished
with herbs.

Baked Spaghetti Squash

One squash makes an excellent side dish for four, served with herb butter.

Serves 4

INGREDIENTS
1 medium spaghetti squash
115 g/4 oz/½ cup butter
45 ml/3 tbsp chopped fresh mixed herbs,
    such as parsley, chives and oregano
1 garlic clove, crushed
1 shallot, chopped
5 ml/1 tsp lemon juice
50 g/2 oz/⅔ cup grated Parmesan cheese
salt and freshly ground black pepper

1 Preheat the oven to 180°C/350°F/ Gas 4. Cut the squash in half lengthways. Place the halves, cut-side down, in a roasting tin. Pour a little water around them, then bake for about 40 minutes until tender.

2 Meanwhile, put the butter, herbs, garlic, shallot and lemon juice in a food processor, and process until thoroughly blended and creamy in consistency. Season to taste.

3 When the squash is tender, scrape out any seeds and cut a thin slice from the base of each half, so that they will sit level. Place the squash halves on warmed serving plates.

4 Using a fork, pull out a few of the spaghetti-like strands in the centre of each. Add a dollop of herb butter, then sprinkle with a little of the grated Parmesan. Serve the remaining herb butter and Parmesan separately, adding them as you pull out more strands.

Baked Marrow in Parsley Sauce

Try to find a small, firm and unblemished marrow for this recipe, as the flavour will be sweet, fresh and delicate.

Serves 4

INGREDIENTS

1 small young marrow, about 900 g/2 lb
30 ml/2 tbsp olive oil
15 g/½ oz/1 tbsp butter
1 onion, chopped
15 ml/1 tbsp plain flour
300 ml/½ pint/1¼ cups milk and single
    cream mixed
30 ml/2 tbsp chopped
    fresh parsley
salt and freshly ground
    black pepper

1 Preheat the oven to 180°C/350°F/ Gas 4 and cut the marrow into pieces measuring about 5 x 2.5 cm/2 x 1 in, leaving the skin intact.

2 Heat the olive oil and butter in a flameproof casserole and fry the chopped onion over a gentle heat until soft but not browned.

3 Add the marrow and sauté for 1–2 minutes. Stir in the flour and cook for a few minutes, then stir in the milk and cream mixture.

4 Add the parsley and seasoning, stir well, cover and cook in the oven for 30–35 minutes. If liked, remove the lid for the final 5 minutes of cooking to brown the top. Alternatively, serve the marrow in its rich, pale sauce.

COOK'S TIP: If you have to use a mature marrow, it will need peeling; young marrows have tender skin and can be cooked unpeeled.

VARIATIONS: Chopped fresh basil or a mixture of basil and chervil also tastes good in this dish. Large courgettes can be used, if liked.

Courgettes & Asparagus en Papillote

These puffed paper parcels should be broken open at the table so that the wonderful aroma can be fully appreciated.

Serves 4

INGREDIENTS
2 medium courgettes
1 medium leek
225 g/8 oz young asparagus
4 fresh tarragon sprigs
4 garlic cloves, unpeeled
1 egg, beaten
salt and freshly ground
    black pepper

2 Trim the asparagus and cut evenly into 5 cm/2 in lengths.

3 Cut out four 30 x 38 cm/ 12 x 15 in sheets of greaseproof paper and fold in half. Draw a large curve to make a heart shape when unfolded. Cut along the inside of the line.

1 Preheat the oven to 200°C/400°F/ Gas 6. Trim the courgettes and, using a potato peeler, slice them lengthways into thin ribbons. Trim the leek and cut into very fine julienne strips.

COOK'S TIP: For julienne strips, use a sharp knife to cut the leek into 7.5 cm/3 in lengths. Cut in half lengthways, then cut into fine, lengthways strips.

4 Divide the courgettes, asparagus and leek evenly between each paper heart, positioning the filling on one side of the fold line and topping each with a sprig of tarragon and an unpeeled garlic clove. Season to taste.

5 Brush the edges of the greaseproof paper lightly with the beaten egg and fold over. Pleat the edges together so that each vegetable parcel is completely sealed. Lay the parcels on a large baking sheet and bake for 10 minutes. Place the four parcels on warmed individual plates, and serve immediately.

Creamed Courgettes au Gratin

A crunchy breadcrumb topping completes this tasty dish.

Serves 4–6

INGREDIENTS
6 courgettes, about 200 g/7 oz each
65 g/2½ oz/5 tbsp unsalted butter
1 onion, finely chopped
60 ml/4 tbsp day-old breadcrumbs
salt and freshly ground black pepper
olives, lemon slices and 1 fresh parsley
    sprig, to garnish

1 Trim the courgettes and cut into
1 cm/½ in slices. Add to a pan of
boiling water and cook for 5–8 minutes
or until tender. Drain very well.

2 Using a potato masher, mash the
courgettes, or blend them in a food
processor or blender, until smooth.

3 Melt 40 g/1½ oz/3 tbsp of the
butter in a frying pan and cook the
onion until soft, then stir in the puréed
courgettes. Cook without browning
for a further 2–3 minutes. Season and
spoon into a warmed ovenproof dish.

4 Dot the puréed courgettes with the
remaining butter and sprinkle over
the breadcrumbs. Cook under a
preheated grill until golden brown.
Garnish with olives, lemon slices and
a sprig of parsley just before serving.

VARIATION: As an alternative,
replace the courgettes with two
large marrows that have been
peeled, seeded and diced.

Courgettes with Moroccan Spices

This goes equally well with a Moroccan or Western-style meal.

Serves 4

INGREDIENTS
500 g/1¼ lb courgettes
lemon juice and chopped fresh coriander
and parsley, to serve

FOR THE SPICY *CHARMOULA*
1 onion
1–2 garlic cloves, crushed
¼ fresh red or green chilli, seeded and
finely sliced
2.5 ml/½ tsp paprika
2.5 ml/½ tsp ground cumin
45 ml/3 tbsp olive oil
salt and freshly ground
black pepper

1 Preheat the oven to 180°C/350°F/
Gas 4. Trim the courgettes and cut
into quarters or eighths lengthways,
depending on their size. Place in a
shallow ovenproof dish or casserole.

2 Finely chop the onion and blend
with the other *charmoula* ingredients
and 60 ml/4 tbsp water. Pour over the
courgettes. Cover with foil and cook
in the oven for about 15 minutes.

3 Baste the courgettes with the
charmoula and return to the oven,
uncovered, for 5–10 minutes until they
are tender. Sprinkle with lemon juice
and fresh herbs, and serve.

Stewed Pumpkin in Coconut Cream

Use the firm-textured Japanese kabocha squash for this dish, if you can.

Serves 4–6

INGREDIENTS
1 kg/2¼ lb kabocha squash
750 ml/1¼ pint/3 cups coconut milk
175 g/6 oz/scant 1 cup granulated sugar
pinch of salt
toasted squash seed kernels and fresh mint
   sprigs, to decorate

2 Pour the coconut milk into a saucepan and add the sugar and salt. Bring to the boil, stirring constantly.

1 Wash the squash skin and, using a sharp knife, cut off most of it. Scoop out the seeds and discard. Cut the flesh into pieces about 5 cm/2 in long and 2 cm/¾ in thick.

3 Add the squash to the coconut milk. Simmer for about 10–15 minutes until the squash is tender.

COOK'S TIP: Any firm-textured pumpkin or squash can be used for this dish. Jamaican or New Zealand Crown Prince or turban varieties make good alternatives to kabocha.

4 Divide among warmed individual serving plates and decorate each one with a few toasted squash seed kernels and a mint sprig. Serve.

VARIATION: Baked pumpkin or squash seeds also make good nibbles.

American Pumpkin Pie

This spicy, sweet pie is traditionally served at Thanksgiving, or at Hallowe'en to use the pulp from the hollowed-out pumpkin lanterns.

Serves 8

INGREDIENTS
200 g/7 oz/1¾ cups plain flour
2.5 ml/½ tsp salt
90 g/3½ oz/7 tbsp unsalted butter
1 egg yolk

FOR THE FILLING
900 g/2 lb pumpkin
2 large eggs
75 g/3 oz/6 tbsp light brown sugar
60 ml/4 tbsp golden syrup
250 ml/8 fl oz/1 cup double cream
15 ml/1 tbsp ground mixed spice
2.5 ml/½ tsp salt
icing sugar, for dusting

1 Sift the flour and salt into a mixing bowl. Rub in the butter until the mixture resembles breadcrumbs, then mix in the egg yolk and enough iced water (about 15 ml/1 tbsp) to make a dough. Roll the dough into a ball, wrap it in clear film and chill it for at least 30 minutes.

2 To make the filling, peel the pumpkin and discard the seeds. Cut the flesh into cubes. Place in a large, heavy-based saucepan, add water to cover and simmer until tender. Mash until completely smooth, then leave in a sieve set over a bowl to drain thoroughly.

3 Roll out the pastry on a lightly floured surface and use it to line a 23–25 cm/9–10 in loose-bottomed flan tin. Prick the base and line with greaseproof paper and baking beans. Chill for 15 minutes.

4 Preheat the oven to 200°C/400°F/ Gas 6. Bake the pastry flan case for 10 minutes, then remove the greaseproof paper and baking beans and bake for 5 minutes more. Remove from the oven and lower the oven temperature to 190°C/375°F/Gas 5.

5 Tip the pumpkin pulp into a bowl and beat in the eggs, sugar, syrup, cream, mixed spice and salt. Pour the mixture into the pastry case. Bake for 40 minutes or until the filling has set. Serve at room temperature, dusted with icing sugar.

Pumpkin Spice Bread

A moist, sweet loaf with a buttery glaze and chopped pecan nut topping.

Makes 1 loaf

INGREDIENTS

2 sachets active dried yeast
250 ml/8 fl oz/1 cup lukewarm water
10 ml/2 tsp ground cinnamon
5 ml/1 tsp ground ginger
5 ml/1 tsp ground allspice
1.5 ml/¼ tsp ground cloves
5 ml/1 tsp salt
120 ml/4 fl oz/½ cup milk
225 g/8 oz/1 cup cooked and
    mashed pumpkin
225 g/8 oz/generous 1 cup sugar
115 g/4 oz/½ cup butter, melted
625 g/1 lb 6 oz/5½ cups flour
50 g/2 oz/½ cup pecan nuts,
    finely chopped

1 In the bowl of an electric mixer, combine the yeast and water, stir and leave for 15 minutes to dissolve. In another bowl, mix the spices together and set aside.

2 To the yeast, add the salt, milk, pumpkin, 90 g/3½ oz/½ cup of the sugar, 45 ml/3 tbsp of the butter, 10 ml/2 tsp of the spice mixture and 225 g/8 oz/2 cups of the flour. Mix well. Gradually mix in the remaining flour to form a rough dough.

COOK'S TIP: If the cooked pumpkin seems too moist, drain it in a sieve.

3 Transfer the dough to a floured surface and knead until smooth. Place in a bowl, cover and leave to rise in a warm place for 1–1½ hours until doubled in bulk.

4 Knock back the dough with your clenched fist and knead briefly. Divide the dough into thirds and roll each one into a 45 cm/18 in rope. Cut each rope into 16 equal pieces, then roll into balls.

5 Grease a 25 cm/10 in ring mould. Stir the remaining sugar into the remaining spice mixture. Roll the balls in the remaining melted butter, then in the spice mixture.

6 Arrange half the balls in the mould and sprinkle over half the pecan nuts. Arrange the remaining balls in the same way but staggering the rows, and sprinkle over the remaining pecan nuts. Cover and leave to rise in a warm place for 45 minutes until almost doubled in bulk.

7 Preheat the oven to 180°C/350°F/ Gas 4. Bake for 55 minutes. Cool in the mould for 20 minutes, then turn out. Serve warm.

VARIATION: Pistachio nuts or hazel nuts could be substituted for the pecan nuts, if you like.

Pumpkin Muffins

To keep these muffins light, fold in the dry ingredients very briefly.

Makes 14

INGREDIENTS

115 g/4 oz/½ cup butter or margarine,
    at room temperature
175 g/6 oz/¾ cup dark brown sugar,
    firmly packed
115 g/4 oz/⅓ cup molasses
1 egg, at room temperature, beaten
225 g/8 oz/1 cup cooked and
    mashed pumpkin
200 g/7 oz/1¾ cups flour
1.5 ml/¼ tsp salt
5 ml/1 tsp baking powder
7.5 ml/1½ tsp ground cinnamon
5 ml/1 tsp freshly grated nutmeg
50 g/2 oz/¼ cup currants
    or raisins

1 Preheat the oven to 200°C/400°F/ Gas 6. Grease 14 muffin tins or use paper cases. Cream the butter or margarine until soft. Add the sugar and molasses and beat until light and fluffy.

2 Add the egg and mashed pumpkin and stir until well blended. Sift over the flour, salt, baking powder, cinnamon and nutmeg. Fold just enough to blend; do not overmix. Fold in the currants or raisins.

3 Spoon the batter into the prepared tins or cases, filling them three-quarters full. Bake for 12–15 minutes until the tops spring back when touched lightly. Serve warm or cold.

Courgette Yeast Bread

Makes 1 loaf

INGREDIENTS
450 g/1 lb/2⅔ cups grated courgettes
30 ml/2 tbsp salt
1 sachet active dried yeast
300 ml/½ pint/1¼ cups
   lukewarm water
400 g/14 oz/3½ cups flour
olive oil, for brushing

1 In a colander, alternate layers of grated courgettes and salt. Leave to drain for 30 minutes, then squeeze out the moisture with your hands. Combine the yeast with 50 ml/2 fl oz/ ¼ cup of the lukewarm water, stir and leave for 15 minutes or until a froth appears on the surface.

2 Mix the courgettes, yeast and flour in a bowl. Add enough of the remaining water to form a rough dough. Transfer to a floured surface and knead until smooth and elastic.

3 Return the dough to the bowl, cover and leave to rise in a warm place for about 1½ hours until doubled in bulk. Knock back the dough and knead into a tapered cylinder.

4 Place on a greased baking sheet, cover and leave to rise in a warm place for about 45 minutes until doubled in bulk. Preheat the oven to 220°C/ 425°F/Gas 7. Brush the dough with olive oil and bake for 40–45 minutes until golden. Cool on a wire rack.

Courgette & Double-ginger Cake

Both fresh and preserved ginger are used to flavour this unusual tea bread. It is delicious served warm, cut into thick slices and spread with butter.

Serves 8–10

INGREDIENTS

3 eggs
225 g/8 oz/generous 1 cup caster sugar
250 ml/8 fl oz/1 cup sunflower oil
5 ml/1 tsp vanilla essence
15 ml/1 tbsp syrup from a jar of
    stem ginger
225 g/8 oz/1⅓ cups grated courgettes
2.5 cm/1 in piece fresh root ginger, peeled
    and grated
350 g/12 oz/3 cups unbleached
    plain flour
5 ml/1 tsp baking powder
pinch of salt
5 ml/1 tsp ground cinnamon
2 pieces stem ginger, chopped
15 ml/1 tbsp demerara sugar

1 Preheat the oven to 190°C/375°F/ Gas 5. Lightly grease a 900 g/2 lb loaf tin. Beat together the eggs and sugar until light and fluffy.

2 Slowly beat the sunflower oil into the egg mixture to form a smooth batter. Mix in the vanilla essence and stem ginger syrup, then stir in the courgettes and fresh ginger.

3 Sift together the flour, baking powder and salt into a large bowl, raising the sieve as high as possible to incorporate more air. Add the ground cinnamon and mix well, then gently stir the dried ingredients into the courgette mixture.

4 Pour the courgette mixture into the prepared tin. Smooth and level the top, then sprinkle the chopped ginger and demerara sugar over the surface.

5 Bake for 1 hour until a skewer inserted into the centre comes out clean. Leave the cake in the tin to cool for about 20 minutes, then turn out on to a wire rack.

This edition is published by Southwater

Southwater is an imprint of
Anness Publishing Ltd
Hermes House
88-89 Blackfriars Road,
London SE1 8HA
tel. 020 7401 2077
fax 020 7633 9499

Distributed in the UK by
The Manning Partnership
251–253 London Road East
Batheaston
Bath BA1 7RL
tel. 01225 852 727
fax 01225 852 852

Distributed in the USA by
Anness Publishing Inc.
27 West 20th Street
Suite 504, New York NY 10011
tel. 212 807 6739
fax 212 807 6813

Distributed in Australia by
Sandstone Publishing
Unit 1, 360 Norton Street,
Leichhardt
New South Wales 2040
tel. 02 9560 7888
fax 02 9560 7488

Publisher: Joanna Lorenz
Editor: Valerie Ferguson
Series Designer: Bobbie Colgate Stone
Designer: Andrew Heath
Production Controller: Joanna King

Recipes contributed by: Catherine Atkinson,
Michelle Berriedale-Johnson, Angela Boggiano,
Carla Capalbo, Kit Chan, Jacqueline Clark,
Trish Davies, Roz Denny, Patrizia Diemling,
Matthew Drennan, Christine France,
Silvano Franco, Shirley Gill, Nicola Graimes,
Rosamund Grant, Rebekah Hassan,
Christine Ingram, Patricia Lousada, Lesley Mackley,
Norma Macmillan, Norma Miller, Sallie Morris,
Annie Nichols, Liz Trigg, Steven Wheeler,
Jeni Wright.
Photography: William Adams-Lingwood,
Karl Adamson, James Duncan, Ian Garlick,
Michelle Garrett, John Heseltine,
Amanda Heywood.

1 3 5 7 9 10 8 6 4 2

Notes:
For all recipes, quantities are given in both metric
and imperial measures and, where appropriate,
measures are also given in standard cups
and spoons.
Follow one set, but not a mixture, because they
are not interchangeable.

Standard spoon and cup measures are level.

1 tsp = 5 ml   1 tbsp = 15 ml

1 cup = 250 ml/8 fl oz

Australian standard tablespoons are 20 ml.
Australian readers should use 3 tsp in place of
1 tbsp for measuring small quantities of gelatine,
cornflour, salt etc.

Medium eggs are used unless otherwise stated.

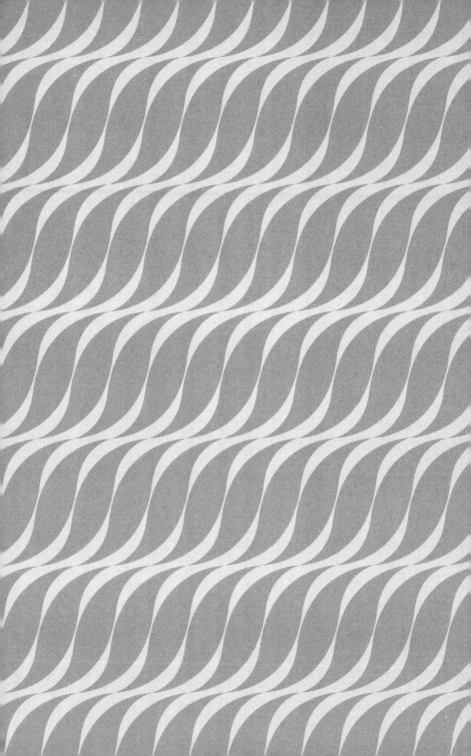